MY CAT

How to Have a Happy, Healthy Pet

First published in the U.S.A. in 2001 by
NorthWord Press
5900 Green Oak Drive
Minnetonka, MN 55343
1-800-328-3895

ISBN 1-55971-792-0

This edition edited by Barbara K. Harold

A catalog record for this book is available from the
Library of Congress, Washington, DC.

Color reproduction by Sang Choy, Singapore
Printed by Kyodo Printing Co. (S'pore) Pte Ltd
Printed in Singapore

10 9 8 7 6 5 4 3 2 1

Conceived and produced by Weldon Owen Pty Limited
59 Victoria Street, McMahons Point, NSW, 2060, Australia
A member of the Weldon Owen Group of Companies
Sydney • San Francisco • London

Weldon Owen Pty Ltd
Publisher: Sheena Coupe
Associate Publisher: Lynn Humphries
Senior Designer: Kylie Mulquin
Editorial Coordinator: Tracey Gibson
Editorial Assistant: Marney Richardson
Production Manager: Helen Creeke
Production Coordinator: Kylie Lawson
Vice President International Sales: Stuart Laurence

Project Editor and Text: Lynn Cole
Consultant: Paul McGreevy, B.V.Sc., Ph.D., M.R.C.V.S.
Illustrator: Janet Jones
Commissioned Photography: Stuart Bowey, Ad-Libitum

Credits and Acknowledgments

[t=top, b=bottom, l=left, r=right]

All photographs by **Stuart Bowey, Ad-Libitum** except: **AGE Fotostock** 47cr. **Bruce Coleman Collection** 19b (J. Burton). **Chanan Photography** 8, 9, 10, 44tr, 47tl, 47bl. **Corbis Images** 1c, 6t, 7t, 16tr, 24r, 36br, 45tl, 45bl, 45cr, 46tl, 46b. **PhotoDisc** 11c, 12tr, 12cr, 41tr. **photolibrary.com** 32tl, 44cl (Photo Researchers Inc.), 31tl, 40tr (Tony Stone Images).

Weldon Owen would like to thank the following people for their assistance in the preparation of this book: Sarah Anderson; Sally and Lucy Bell and "Spike"; Eliza and Jess Bowey and "Sao"; Jean-Pierre Buisson and "Clicquot"; Karen Burgess and "Tao"; Cat Protection Society of NSW; Dean Chittick and "Lily"; Mahalia Christel-Gensen; Peta Gorman; Michael Hann; Sam Haynes and Kathy Stone of Sydney Animal Hospitals, Newtown; Danniella Harrison and "Ginger"; Eva Krynda and Holly Bourne and Korat litter; Lena Lowe and "Ferro"; Pamela Miller and Ruby Charlton and Burmese litter; Edward and Oliver Minnet and "Bacci"; Kylie Mulquin and "Channi" and "Pascal"; Margaret and Kris Papadatos and "Rosie", "Faith," and "Paris"; Marney Richardson and "Jasmine"; Alexander Roche and "Kirime"; Jack Staniford.

MY CAT

How to Have a Happy, Healthy Pet

NorthWord Press
Minnetonka, Minnesota

Contents

Which cat should you choose? 6

Where to get a cat or kitten 12

What to buy before your cat comes home 14

Creating a safe environment 16

Bringing your new cat home 18

House-training your cat 20

Feeding your cat 22

Grooming your cat 24

Handling your cat 28

Playing with your cat   30

Traveling with your cat   34

When your cat can't go with you   36

Regular health checks   38

Visiting the vet   40

Having kittens   42

Why does my cat do the things it does?   44

Index   48

Which cat should you choose?

Cats make great pets. They easily adapt to family life and fit into any size home. This book will help you get off to a good start with your new pet. While you help it understand the rules in your house, you will be making a very special friend for life! On the following pages you will meet just a few of the most popular cat breeds.

Safer inside

Cats, like this domestic shorthair, don't mind living indoors. If you live near a busy road, this is the safest place for your new pet. Most cats love to watch what's going on from somewhere up high—window ledges are perfect.

Choosing from the litter

Spend some time watching kittens, like these Korats, playing together or with their mother. Ask if you may touch the mother—if she seems friendly, the kittens are likely to be, too. Both males and females make good pets. It's your decision. A kitten that cuddles and purrs, and seems to want to be friends with you, will be the best one to choose.

Two's company

If your cat will be alone for part of the day, it might be a good idea to have two cats. Cats of the opposite sex will probably get along well with each other. Cats of the same sex may fight. Littermates, like these two domestic shorthairs, may be more interested in playing with each other than with you, which may not be what you want in a pet.

Being a good owner

You must make your home safe for your new cat. And the yard, too, if it is to be allowed outside. Longhairs need more grooming than others, so maybe a shorthaired cat is better for you than a Persian or other longhaired breed. Remember to see that your cat always has fresh water. (There are less pleasant jobs to be done, too, such as cleaning the litter box.) Remember that cats, like this domestic shorthair, often live for 16 years or more. All cats should get a microchip for identification. And you may want to have your cat neutered, which means that it can't have kittens.

Purebred...

Purebred cats come in a huge range of body shapes, coat types, and an enormous choice of solid colors and color combinations.

Personality Loving, quiet, shy
Place to live Indoor/outdoor
Coat and color Longhair (the coat is up to 6 inches/15 cm long). Comes in all colors, color combinations, and patterns
Grooming Be prepared to spend lots of time every day combing and brushing the long coat so it doesn't get tangled
Note Tabby is a patterned coat with striped or blotchy markings

Maine Coon
(black and white)

Personality Energetic, good-natured, and talkative
Place to live Indoor/outdoor
Coat and color The thick, long coat comes in all colors, color combinations, and patterns, except colorpointed
Grooming Brush lightly every few days to remove dead hairs
Note: Colorpointed cats have a darker color fur on their "points"– the face, ears, legs, and tail

Persian
(brown tabby)

Exotic Shorthair
(red tabby)

Personality Quiet, loyal, and playful
Place to live Indoor/outdoor
Coat and color The short coat comes in all colors, color combinations, and patterns, except colorpointed
Grooming Brush and comb twice a week to remove dead hairs
Note: It is impossible to tell if a young kitten of this breed will have a long or short coat

Personality Lively and loving
Place to live Indoor
Coat and color The short coat is mostly pale with darker face, ears, feet, and tail in various colors, including blue, chocolate, seal point, lilac, or red
Grooming Brush and comb twice a week to remove dead hairs
Note: These cats are great "talkers," and their wails can sound like babies crying

Siamese
(seal point)

Personality Loving, playful, and curious

Place to live Indoor/outdoor

Coat and color The sleek, short coat comes in red, blue, and tan. Each hair has three bands of color with a dark tip.

Grooming Comb the coat regularly to remove loose hairs. Wipe with a damp cloth to make the coat shine

Abyssinian
(ruddy)

Oriental Shorthair
(ebony and silver tabby)

Personality Intelligent and loving. Enjoys human company

Place to live Indoor

Coat and color Short fine coat. Comes in all colors, color combinations, and patterns. (Also a Longhair type)

Grooming Comb regularly to remove loose hairs, and wipe over with a damp cloth to make the coat shine

Note: Best fed a low-fat diet

Personality Quiet, loving, and good-natured

Place to live Indoor/outdoor

Coat and color Longhair and Shorthair. Comes in all colors, color combinations, and patterns, except colorpoints

Grooming Brush and comb both long and short coats regularly to remove dead hairs

Note: The ears should fold forward and sit like a rounded cap

Personality Gentle, loving, playful, and intelligent

Place to live Indoor/outdoor

Coat and color Longhair and Shorthair. Has a pale body color, with darker face, ears, legs, and tail in various colors—gold, blue, seal point, lilac, or chocolate. The feet should be white

Grooming Brush and comb both long and short coats regularly to remove dead hairs

Birman
(seal point)

Scottish Fold
(red tabby and white)

**Devon Rex
(red tabby)**

Personality Very affectionate and loves to sit on your lap
Place to live Indoor
Coat and color Its unusual, very short wavy coat feels like suede. Comes in all colors, color combinations, and patterns
Grooming Gently comb every day, and smooth over with a silk cloth or your hand. Clean inside the large ears with damp cotton balls

Personality Friendly, loving, and independent
Place to live Indoor/outdoor —an excellent hunter
Coat and color Short, thick, coarse coat. Comes in all colors, color combinations, and patterns
Grooming Comb regularly to remove loose hairs, and wipe over with a damp cloth to make the coat shine

**American
Shorthair
(silver tabby)**

Personality Loves the company of people and will follow you around
Place to live Indoor
Coat and color Shorthair. Comes in about ten colors. All have darker points on face, ears, feet, and tail
Grooming Comb once a week, and wipe with a damp cloth to make the coat shine

Personality Very affectionate and easy to train. Doesn't like to be left alone too much
Place to live Indoor
Coat and color Shorthair. Body colors may be white to bronze, patterned with darker spots, like a wild ocelot, and lines around neck and legs
Grooming Give the coat a quick comb and brush every day, and wipe with a damp cloth

**Ocicat
(chocolate)**

**Burmese
(sable)**

10

...or mixed breed?

Domestic cats come in every color and combination of colors, longhaired or short, that you can imagine. The main thing is that you choose a loving and playful pet, one that likes to be stroked and held.

Domestic shorthair
(tabby markings)
Tabby is the word used to describe a patterned coat with round, striped, or blotchy markings

Domestic longhair
(tabby markings)

Domestic shorthair
(tortoiseshell and white)

Domestic shorthair
(solid color)

Persian cross
(blue and white markings)

Where to get a cat or kitten

Kittens may also be found through friends or advertisements in newspapers

Written pedigrees are really only important to breeders or people who want to win ribbons at cat shows. When you decide on a particular type of cat, you may want to find a good breeder who specializes in that breed. If you are not so concerned about the breed, many animal shelters have well-trained staff who can help you find a cat that's perfect for you.

Ears should be clean and not smelly

Eyes should be bright and not watery or sticky

Animal shelters

These are good places to find a cat or kitten, like this domestic shorthair, and there are lots to choose from. These cats have been checked over by a vet to make sure they are healthy, and are already neutered and vaccinated. The cost to adopt from a shelter is usually far less than to buy from a breeder.

Nose should be moist, cool, and not running

Mouth should have pink gums and breath should smell clean

Domestic shorthair kitten

Paperwork

When you buy your new pet, the breeder or shelter should give you all the kitten's papers, fully completed. These include:

- Pedigree papers
- Certificates for all vaccinations
- A record of its microchip number and the form for providing your address
- Written advice on worming and on any other vaccinations your new pet needs
- A diet sheet showing what type of food the kitten is used to and offering some advice on its future diet. (Some breeders will even give you some of the food your kitten has been eating.)

The fur should be shiny and clean

Kitten should move freely on all four paws

The breeder

You may want to buy a kitten, like one of these 8-week-old Burmese, from a breeder. The place where the cats are kept should be fresh and clean, and they should have plenty of space. Always ask to see the mother if she is not with the kittens.

Your kitten's health

Kittens are ready to leave their mother when they are 6 to 8 weeks old. The kitten you choose should be bright-eyed and friendly. This domestic shorthair looks perfect, but it's a good idea to have any new pet checked over by your vet within the first few days.

What to buy before your cat comes home

Wicker basket

Bean bag

Cat sock

Shopping for your new cat is fun! You can get ready for your cat to join your family by having everything it will need to feel comfortable and at home. Cats are likely to be scared in strange surroundings, so you will need a travel cage for the car ride home.

Bedding

Your cat needs somewhere warm and dry to sleep. It will feel safer if you put its bed up off the floor. Pet stores have many kinds of beds to choose from. But no matter how nice you make the bed, some cats and kittens would rather find their own place to sleep.

Make your own kitten bed

If you don't want a bed from a pet store, you can make your own. First, find a box the right size, cut off the flaps, and cut a piece out of one side so the kitten can get in and out easily. Next, line the box with clean newspapers and something soft (such as an old towel or sweater). Finally, put the bed in a warm, quiet place not too far from your cat's litter box and water bowl.

Collars and tags

Your cat should have a microchip for identification. If it will be outdoors, it should also wear a tag on its collar with your address and phone number. Collars with an elastic strip are the safest. Perhaps a small bell on the collar is also a good idea—birds will be able to hear when the cat is near them.

Ceramic dish

Non-slip metal bowl

Metal bowl

Bowls

It's best to choose flat dishes, or bowls that are wide enough not to catch your cat's whiskers. Check that they won't slip or tip over. Make sure your cat always has a bowl of fresh water.

Organic litter

Clumping litter

Recycled newspaper litter

Scratching post

Cats that live outdoors often scratch at rough tree trunks to let other cats know that they live nearby. An indoor cat will scratch at furniture in the same way unless you teach it to use a scratching post. The best kind of post has a wide base, so it won't fall over on your cat.

Litter and box

Cats are naturally clean, so it's easy to train them to use a litter box if they can't be outside. Put the box somewhere quiet, and clean it out often. Your cat won't like the smell of a dirty box any more than you will! Plastic liners (or newspaper) and scoopable litter make the job of cleaning the box easier.

Creating a safe environment

Before you bring your new pet home, check through your house as if you were the cat. Dangling blind cords, for example, or power cables look like toys to cats, but they could be dangerous. Make sure the windows can be closed securely. And close off rooms where your cat might knock over things that could break!

Safe nap spot
Once your cat settles into its new home, you will find it curled up in all kinds of cozy corners, as this domestic shorthair has done. Cats like to sleep a lot, so you may often find your pet napping! Try to wake a sleeping cat gently.

Using a scratching post
This Burmese has learned to use a scratching post instead of the couch to sharpen its claws. If your cat starts to stretch and claw at the furniture, say "No" and quickly take it to the post. You could put its paws gently on the post to show it how nice and rough the surface is. Or you could rub the post with Catnip. Cats love the smell of this plant and will go to it quickly and happily.

Cat flaps

Your cat can go outside if you have made your yard a safe place. This domestic longhair comes and goes as it likes through a cat flap. You will not have to worry about a litter box, except at night, when it's safest to keep your cat indoors.

Enclosed cat run

This Korat has a large and safe outdoor run. Here it can jump, and prowl, and play. Cats especially like being able to climb up high where they can see everything that's going on.

Cat-proofing your home

Medicines meant for people, even ones we think of as safe, such as aspirin, are very bad for cats. All medicines, and kitchen and bathroom cleansers should be locked away. Poisonous things used in the garden should also be kept in a safe place. And don't forget the car antifreeze—it belongs out of reach in the garage. Cats like to explore new things and places. For example, kittens can fall into the toilet and drown, so everyone in your family must remember to leave the lid closed, or keep the bathroom door shut. Try to think of every way you can to make your home as safe as possible for your new pet.

Bringing your new cat home

It is a good idea to let your pet get used to its new home slowly. You may like to keep it in just one or two rooms for a few days. To get to know your cat you can get down on the floor with it and let it smell your hand. Speak quietly and call it by its name. The cat should meet other members of the family in the same way. Cats like to be stroked gently from head to tail. They will sometimes start to purr as they relax.

A safe trip
This domestic shorthair has a special box for riding in the car. The door latches securely to keep the cat safely inside. That way, it can't run out into danger if someone opens a car door without thinking.

Your cat's corner
Sometimes your home is very busy. People rush around in the morning or when making dinner at night. These are good times to put your kitten on its bed in its own corner. This domestic shorthair is safely out of the way and it will be less frightened while it gets used to the noise of its new home.

Meeting the family

Everyone will want to meet your new pet, but don't let them all rush in together. They should get down to the cat's level, as the new owners of this domestic longhair are doing. They should speak quietly, and let the cat come to them as it chooses. Don't let family or friends pick the cat up until they have been shown how to hold it properly (see page 28).

Meeting your dog

Make sure the cat can't get out of the house in a panic. You should hold your dog tightly, **not** the cat. The cat will probably fluff itself up, hiss, spit, and run away. Don't let the dog chase the cat. Try to get the dog's attention away from the cat. You could shake a noisy toy when it glances away from the cat. Repeat the meetings until the two get used to each other.

Meeting your other cat

The first few times any two cats meet, put the new cat in its cage and let the older cat get used to its smell. The next step is to put their food out at the same time with their bowls a little way apart and let them eat together. If they start to fight, take the newer cat away and try again at the next meal.

House-training your cat

Your new kitten will have already learned lots of useful things from its mother, but it doesn't know the rules in your home. Cats love to please people, which is one reason people and cats get along so well. You can train your cat by letting it know when it has done the right thing. Reward it with food treats and hugs (if that's what it likes), and talk to it in a soft, happy voice.

Treats

This Australian Mist is getting a food treat because its owner is pleased with it. The treat can be anything your cat really likes, such as a piece of cheese, meat, or fish, or cat treats from the store—these smell especially good to cats.

Teaching the rules

Your cat should never be allowed to jump onto kitchen counters where food is prepared. Say "No" firmly, and take the cat away from the area. The laundry room is not a safe place for cats, so you should teach your cat to stay away from there, too. (Even better, keep the door closed.) Until your cat is fully trained to use its litter box, it may have an occasional accident, so keep it off the furniture—especially your bed—until it learns where to do its "job." If your cat has an accident, don't be angry. Just clean and rinse the area thoroughly—if the smell is still there, the cat might use the same place as a toilet again.

The litter box

Take your kitten to the litter box as soon as it wakes up, or has eaten its food. Let it be alone and quiet, like this Korat, while it goes to the toilet. If it looks as if it wants to "go" at other times, quickly take it to the litter box again and wait quietly. Change the litter often so it doesn't get smelly. Always wash your hands after you touch the box. If you close the doors to other parts of the house, the kitten may learn to use the box more quickly.

Praising and rewarding

Not all cats are easy to train, so you need to be patient! Some cats are happiest when they are being fed, while others like to be left alone. Most cats like to be petted, like this Persian crossbred. Always talk to your cat in a quiet voice, and **never** hit your cat.

Smells cats don't like

Orange peel has a smell cats don't like, so you can use it to teach your cat to keep away from places you don't want it to go. Even just a small piece may do the trick!

Feeding your cat

Dry food

Young kittens are fed by their mothers whenever they are hungry, so when you bring your kitten home, give it small meals often. As your pet grows bigger, it will eat more food but less often. To see how much food your cat should have at each meal, read the label, or ask your vet to help you. And make sure there is always plenty of fresh drinking water.

Canned cat food

Fresh sardines

Treats from the store

Cheese as a treat

Cooked chicken as a treat

Mealtimes
This domestic shorthair is hungry! You can leave dry food out all the time for your cat (unless you have a dog that gobbles it up), but only give your cat as much canned or fresh food as it can eat at each meal. When the cat has finished, take the food away—it gets dry and stale quickly.

Kinds of food
Good-quality dry food made specially for cats has everything your cat needs, and this kind of crunchy food helps to clean its teeth. If your cat starts to get fat, give it less food. Encourage your cat to enjoy different kinds of foods, including fresh chicken or fish. But be sure to ask your vet before you give any new food to your cat.

Dangerous foods

Many cats would like milk or table scraps, but your cat may get sick from them. Don't give your cat cooked bones, because they can splinter into sharp pieces when they are chewed. You should never give cats onions or chocolate, and letting your cat swallow pieces of string or yarn can be dangerous.

Fresh water

Cats that eat dry food will drink more water than those fed on fresh food, but all cats, like this domestic shorthair, need plenty of water. If you have a dog as well as a cat, they can share a water bowl.

Eating together

These two cats, a Burmese and an Australian Mist, happily share a water bowl, but each should have its food served separately. You should wash the cat bowls in the laundry tub, not with dishes the family uses.

Pin-cushion and soft bristle brush

Double-sided comb

Flea combs

Rubber brush

Rubber glove

Grooming your cat

Your cat has its own grooming routine, but a little extra help from you will mean that it won't swallow so many loose hairs. Most of the cat's loose hairs will get caught in your comb or brush instead. Your help is especially important at the end of winter. This is when your cat sheds its thick, warm winter coat to get ready for summer.

Cats like to be clean

If you watch your cat licking itself, as this domestic shorthair is doing, you will notice that it cleans every bit of its body. It does this to get rid of dirt or anything that might have become stuck to its fur.

Grooming tools

Your vet or a professional groomer will help you to choose the tools that are best for your cat's coat type and show you how to use them. It's very important to be gentle so your cat will learn to like the grooming.

Hand grooming

You don't always need to use a comb or brush. Stroking your cat lightly with your hands will remove dead hairs from its coat. It also spreads the natural oils that keep the coat in good condition. Most cats love to be stroked.

Cleaning your cat's eyes

1 Dip a cotton ball in clean, plain water. Squeeze it so it is wet but not dripping with water.

2 Starting from the corner of the eye closest to the nose, wipe down the nose to remove any material that has collected in the corner of the eye.

3 To avoid spreading germs, use a fresh cotton ball to clean the other eye in the same way. If there is yellowish pus in its eyes, you must take your cat to the vet.

25

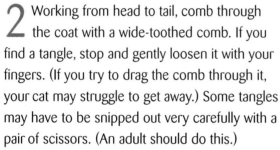

Grooming a longhaired cat

1 It's a good idea to ask a professional groomer to show you how to groom your cat. Before you start, spend a few moments stroking your cat to calm it. Sprinkle a little cornstarch over the coat, and gently rub it in with your fingers—do this a little at a time so you don't make a big cloud of powder. Avoid getting powder in the cat's eyes.

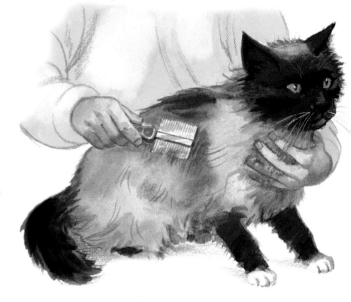

2 Working from head to tail, comb through the coat with a wide-toothed comb. If you find a tangle, stop and gently loosen it with your fingers. (If you try to drag the comb through it, your cat may struggle to get away.) Some tangles may have to be snipped out very carefully with a pair of scissors. (An adult should do this.)

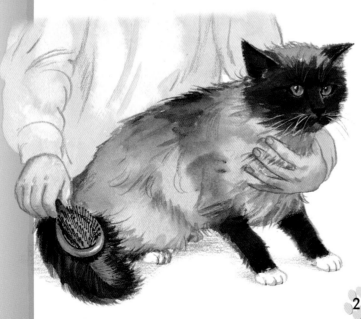

3 The last step is to fluff up the coat with a soft brush. Brushing in the opposite direction—from tail to head—will make the coat stand away from the body so it will look full and fluffy. (You may need someone to help hold your cat, especially when you are grooming the tail.)

Grooming a shorthaired cat

1 If you groom your cat every few days, it will get used to being handled in this way. Using a fine-toothed comb, comb the coat in the direction it grows, from head to tail. Some cats will allow you to comb under their chin and their belly, as well. Use your hand to stroke the legs.

2 To make the coat shine, stroke it with a rubber brush, or a damp cloth, in the direction that the coat grows. Or you can rub it with a silk scarf. (This works especially well on cats with very short coats, such as Ocicats and Oriental Shorthairs.)

Hairballs

If your cat has lost its appetite or is straining when it goes to the toilet, it may have a hairball. These are formed by the hairs it swallows while grooming itself. The cat must cough or vomit the hairball back up. A cat sometimes chews on grass to make this happen, but sometimes it will need help from the vet to get rid of it. The best way to prevent hairballs from forming is by grooming regularly.

Handling your cat

An adult cat can be heavy. If it doesn't want to be picked up, it can be squirmy. The main thing is that the cat should feel safe. Hold it close to your body with one arm around its chest under its front legs. The other hand holds the weight of the body at the tail end. If your cat struggles, let it go, or it may scratch you.

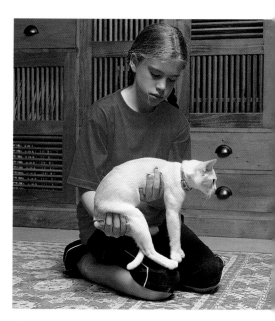

Picking up a cat

To do this, it is a good idea to crouch beside the cat. Next, put one hand around its chest behind the front legs, and gently scoop up the tail end with your other hand. Try not to "twist" the cat as you pick it up. Hold the cat firmly, supporting the body weight (cats like to face you when they are picked up). Never try to pick up an adult cat, like this Burmese, by the scruff of its neck.

Holding a kitten

You can safely pick up a young kitten by the scruff of its neck, the way its mother does, but you must support its weight with your other hand. This domestic shorthair kitten is very happy in its owner's arms. Speak quietly to your kitten as you hold it to calm it.

Training on a leash

Cats don't need to go for walks like dogs do. They get all the exercise they need by playing. But if you start when your pet is a kitten, it may get used to a body harness, like this Burmese kitten is wearing. Then you can take it with you for short walks on a leash.

Sensitive parts

A cat's tail is not a handle—it is part of the cat's backbone. Never pull the tail or grab it during a chasing game, because you might hurt or seriously injure the cat. Always handle your cat's head, eyes, and ears gently, Never pull the ears.

Korat kitten

Rescue tips

If your cat gets stuck up a tree, or is balancing on a high fence or a balcony, stay calm. Don't move toward the cat. Instead, get some food treats and hold them out to the cat. Call its name, and toss some food or a toy in the direction away from the danger. You will need to be calm, and patient, and speak quietly. You may need help from an adult.

Playing with your cat

Toys on an elastic rope

Toys that make noise

Toys filled with catnip

Toy balls

When your cat is playing, it's happy, alert, and full of fun. A cat can make believe that any small thing that moves is something it has to "kill." It may "hunt" a leaf in the garden, or a ball of paper on the kitchen floor, batting and tossing it to keep it moving. The cat may get pretty excited, so remember to keep your hands away from its sharp little claws.

A game of fetch

This Burmese is fetching a toy mouse for its owner. To teach your cat to do this, toss a toy and, when it pounces on the toy, call your cat to you. Don't throw the toy too far. Reward your cat for bringing it back by tossing the toy again immediately.

Kinds of toys

Anything can be a toy to a cat! It's best to buy just a few toys until you find out what games your cat likes best. If you put some of the toys away from time to time, they will seem new when your cat sees them again.

Cats are curious

Cats, like this domestic shorthair, want to know what's making every little sound they hear—and they can hear much better than humans can! This is very important, because sounds tell cats many things. If the cat is inside, for example, it can hear where you are and when its food is ready. If it is outside, its good hearing can warn it of nearby danger.

Make a kitten playhouse

This Korat will have lots of fun hiding and playing in its playhouse. All you have to do is cut some holes in a cardboard box, or a large paper shopping bag (plastic bags are dangerous). If you make scratching noises on the outside, or toss paper balls through the openings, your kitten will have a great time. It will also be getting some exercise and practicing some of the things cats need to be good at.

"Hunting" a scrap of paper

Look at this Abyssinian "hunting." You can see how its ears are pointed forward toward its "prey." And its body looks ready to jump away if the paper ball "attacks." You can tell by the way the tail points straight up and bends over that this cat is happy and is having a good time. Some cats will play this simple game for hours. They chase the paper ball all over the place!

Games with string

Cats love all kinds of games with string. This Burmese might think the string is alive when it wriggles like a snake! It is getting ready to pounce on the string! Or you could tie a toy onto a piece of string and make it move "by magic" from across the room. Always put string toys away when your cat is alone. It could swallow the string, or get caught in it.

Plants cats like

Some cats, especially males like this Burmese, roll around and become very playful when they just smell Catnip. They like to eat it too. You can grow this herb in your garden, or in a pot inside. Cats also like to chew the grass on your lawn. If your cat is kept indoors, you could grow some special grass, called Cat Grass, in a pot. If you keep these two special plants in a separate area, your cat will soon learn that it is allowed to eat them. You can buy both Catnip (*Nepeta cataria*) and Cat Grass (*Dachylis glomerata*) from a plant nursery.

Burmese near Catnip

Australian Mist
chewing Cat Grass

Don't touch

Some plants, such as Poinsettia and Delphinium, are poisonous or can make cats itch. If your cat starts to chew on one of these plants, or rub itself against the plant or the pot, say "No" firmly and carry it away from the area. You can play a game to take your cat's attention away. Soon your cat will learn to stay away from them.

Poinsettia

Delphinium

Traveling with your cat

Cats like to explore, but they usually don't like going on long journeys. If you must take your cat on a trip, your family will need to make careful plans. Try to take the trip when the weather is neither very hot nor very cold. Be sure your pet will have fresh water at regular stops during the journey.

A safe way to travel
This Burmese travels in a cage that lets it see out. This is fine in the car, as long as the cat is not frightened. If it is, it may settle down more quickly if the top is covered with a sheet or a towel. (Make sure your cat can get plenty of air and is not too hot.)

Getting your cat used to a cage
Before your trip, start putting your cat in its traveling cage. Pet your cat gently until it relaxes. Do this a few times every day, as with this Burmese, until it gets used to the idea of being in a small space. Leave it for a little longer each time, but always pet and reward it. You can even get your cat into the habit of having its evening meal in the cage.

Sealable container with litter

Water

Plastic bags

Food

Towel

Travel kit

Your travel gear should include food, water, and a bowl, as well as a first-aid kit with a booklet showing what to do in an emergency. And don't forget plastic bags for cleaning up the litter.

Travel stress

Travel is hard for cats, especially air travel. If you and your family must take a long trip, ask your vet how you can make it easier on your cat. If you are traveling by car and stop overnight on the way, be very careful that your cat doesn't panic in its new surroundings and escape from your room when you let it out of the traveling cage. If you send your pet ahead, make sure there is someone reliable to pick it up at the other end as soon as it arrives. They should understand that the cat will be very distressed by its experience. When you are with your pet again, give it lots of love and attention.

Certified for air travel

Airlines will not accept pets unless they are in a special kind of traveling box like this one. The best thing to do for your cat is to line the bottom of the box with a thick layer of newspaper. Then tear up enough strips to half-fill it. This will keep your cat warm and act like litter if the cat goes to the toilet.

When your cat can't go with you

Cats like their own home best, and they sleep for much of the time anyway. So, a cat that's used to being indoors will be quite all right left alone for a day or so, as long as it has food and water. Your parents should ask a friend to check on the cat. You should always leave the phone number where you will be staying, and your vet's phone number in case of an emergency.

Dry food dispenser

Water dispenser

Food and water dispensers

These automatic dispensers hold enough dry food and water for a couple of days. If your cat usually eats fresh or canned food, make the change to dry food gradually, several days before you leave.

Cat sitters or visitors

This Russian Blue is pleased to see a friend with a food treat. The cat sitter should change the litter and fill the food and water bowls or dispensers. A really good cat sitter will also pet and play with your cat on each visit.

Finding a good cat kennel

If there's no one to look after your cat at home, it can stay at a cat kennel. If you know any other cat owners, ask if they know a good one. Visit it before you take your cat, to make sure that the other animals look clean and happy. Be sure there is plenty of fresh water for them. About a week before you drop your cat off at the kennel, check your records to make sure your pet's vaccinations are up-to-date. Your pet will not be allowed to stay there if its vaccinations are not current.

Boarding cages

Some vets will look after pets while their owners are away. The cages should be large enough for your cat to move around in, and the place where the cages are kept should be clean and airy.

Familiar scent

Your cat will settle better if it has something with it that smells familiar. This domestic longhair has a blanket from its home to comfort it while its owners are away. A toy or an old sweater that smells like you are other things your cat would like.

Regular health checks

Your cat can't tell you when it feels sick, so you must try to be a good detective and notice all the little clues and signs that show there's a problem. Every time you groom your pet, notice anything that's different. Giving your cat these little check-ups will help it to stay healthy.

Flea

Tick

Checking for fleas and ticks

If you see your cat scratching a lot, it may have fleas. (Look for black flea dirt on the skin, as the owner of this Siamese is doing. Because this dirt is partly blood, it will turn red if you wet it on a piece of tissue.) Ticks are most often found on the cat's head and neck. The best way to find them is to run your fingers carefully over every bit of your cat's skin, feeling for tiny lumps. Be sure to look in the ears. Your vet will tell you what to do about these pests.

Checking eyes and ears

Your pet's eyes should look bright and clear, like the eyes of this Burmese. There should be no redness or goo in the corners. If your cat is squinting, take it to the vet—there could be something in its eyes. The inside of your cat's ears should look clean and pink, with no sign of goo. If your cat is shaking its head, or scratching at its ears, or the ears are smelly, sore, or swollen, take it to the vet.

Worming

Several different kinds of worms can live in your cat's body, so it sometimes needs to have medicine to get rid of them. Your vet will help with this. Cat worms can do more harm to humans than they do to cats. So always wash your hands carefully after handling your cat so that you don't get worms from it.

Vaccinations

Injecting a vaccine into an animal is a way of protecting it from diseases it might catch from other animals. Your vet will tell you what vaccinations your cat needs and when it should have them. Then it's up to you to see that your cat gets them. If you don't, your cat could become very ill. You could get a small calendar and make a note on it when each shot is due.

Visiting the vet

Like people, all pets get sick from time to time. Usually it's nothing serious, but just as you sometimes have to see the doctor, your cat sometimes needs some help to get well again. Your cat should also have an annual check-up when it's not sick, so that the vet can be sure your cat is healthy.

Care and kindness

When cats are not well, they may want to sleep even more than usual. This gives them the chance to heal whatever is wrong. All you need to do is to be quiet and gentle with your cat, so it will know you love it. Make sure that water is always available, even if your cat doesn't want to eat. After a day or so it will be ready to play again.

At the vet clinic

It is a good idea to put your cat in a carrying box to take it to see the vet—there will be other animals in the waiting room that might scare it. The vet will check your cat's temperature, ears, eyes, and mouth and ask what signs you have noticed. This is also a good chance for you to ask about anything you want to know about your pet.

We all feel better after a good sleep, and this kitten will, too.

Tell-tale signs

If your cat seems suddenly to be losing weight or putting it on and you haven't changed its food, see your vet. If you notice any of the signs below (**the ones in bold type like this are URGENT**), and the problem goes on for more than a day, see your vet.

- If your cat **seems unusually sleepy**, or doesn't want to play, or is limping, or is **having trouble standing up**
- If it is not interested in food
- If its breath smells awful
- If any part of the body seems sore, or tender, or swollen
- If it is **straining when it tries to go to the toilet**, or it has diarrhea (urgent if **the feces looks bloody**)
- If it vomits more than twice and is not just passing hairballs (urgent if **vomit is bloody or dark**)
- If it seems thirsty all the time

- If it **can't urinate**, or is going more or less often than usual
- If it is drooling or dribbling
- If it is coughing, or **breathing in a strange way**, or **sneezing a lot**
- If it is **squinting**, or there is goo coming from the eyes, or the eyes are red
- If it keeps on scratching, especially at its ears, or shaking its head, or the ears are smelly, or there is goo coming from them
- If it is **pawing at its mouth** (there may be something stuck there)
- If it has a sore that won't heal
- If the fur is flat and the eyes are dull

Having kittens

If your cat has a litter of kittens, your home will be jam-packed full of fun! When they are first born, they will stay close to their mother. No matter how much you want to pick them up and show them to all your friends, you must not. When the mother is ready to "share" them with people, she'll let you know.

Eight-week-old Burmese kitten

The new litter

If your pet is expecting kittens, she will need extra food, and somewhere safe and quiet for her family. There are usually 4 to 6 kittens in a litter, and the mother (called a queen) will be very busy caring for them. Start looking for good homes for the kittens even before they arrive. These Burmese kittens are 11 days old, so they are not ready to go exploring just yet.

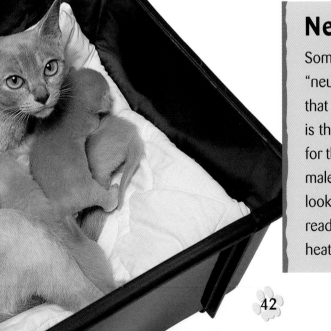

Neutering

Some people have their pet cats "neutered" or "spayed," which means that they can't have kittens. One reason is that it may be hard to find good homes for the kittens. Another reason is that males (called toms) don't wander away looking for females. (When females are ready to mate, they are said to be "in heat," and their smell attracts males.)

42

How kittens grow

When kittens are first born, they are tiny and helpless, and their eyes are closed. The only food they need is their mother's milk. After 7 to 10 days, the eyes open and the kittens start to stumble about on their wobbly legs. Like human babies, they grow very quickly. When they are about 3 weeks old, it will be okay to pick them up and start getting them used to being handled. If you put the litter box nearby, they will quickly learn to use it by watching their mother. After about 4 weeks, they will begin to eat solid food. At about 8 weeks, they can be vaccinated. Then they are ready to go to the new homes you have found for them.

One week old: eyes still closed, sleeps a lot

Three weeks old: can focus its eyes and move around

Six weeks old: active and curious; starting to eat some solid food

Eight weeks old: starting to explore; playful and steady on its feet

43

Why does my cat do the things it does?

Cats can't speak, but they send very clear messages with their bodies in a special code called "body language." By watching your cat closely, you can see if it is happy or angry, hungry or sad. Here are a few examples to help you learn your cat's body language.

Hisses

When your cat hisses and shows its teeth, as this domestic shorthair is doing, it is trying to look fierce enough to scare something–or someone–away. The cat may be really frightened, but it is pretending not to be. Don't touch it, or it might scratch you by accident.

Stretches

When a cat wakes up after a sleep, it always stretches its body, like this Burmese is doing, to get its muscles ready for action. If your cat rolls over on its back, it might be inviting you to stroke its belly. When it's all done stretching, it will be ready to play.

Sniffs at faces

These two Maine Coons are saying "Hello." By sniffing each other's faces they can discover lots of things, such as where the other cat has been, and if either has met any other interesting cats. Cats have an excellent sense of smell, so they can tell a lot more about each other from a sniff than we can.

Climbs the curtains

Kittens, like these domestic shorthairs, love to climb, and curtains are easy targets. The trouble is, it's not so easy for them to get down again without falling and hurting themselves, and the curtains may get scratched. If you see your kitten climbing furniture or curtains, say "No" firmly, and take it to its scratching post, or play a game to get it interested in something else.

Arches its back

This domestic shorthair kitten has seen something scary. It fluffs itself up and turns its side to the object so that it looks bigger than it really is. Its ears are pulled forward, listening. Its back is arched and the legs are stiff so that the kitten can spring away instantly in any direction.

Play-fights

These American Shorthair kittens are practicing their self-defense skills on each other. Although they may hiss and fluff themselves up, they won't hurt each other. It's just a game, and very good exercise for them.

Rubbing against your leg

This domestic shorthair is rubbing against its owner's leg to say a friendly "Hello, here I am." The cat is rubbing its scent onto the leg and picking up some of its owner's scent at the same time.

Hunts and stalks

Cats are hunters—and they don't stop just because they are well fed. This domestic shorthair is watching its target closely as it slowly creeps close enough to pounce. The ears point forward to catch the slightest sound. The head is low and held very steady as the cat steps forward without making a sound. This is just one part of being a cat.

Meows

This domestic shorthair kitten is meowing for attention. Its mother would have responded at once, so now the kitten is seeing if meowing works on its new owner. The kitten is probably feeling hungry, lonely, or upset. Some affection from you will have it purring again in no time!

Your cat is your friend

Everyone likes to be with their friends. Playing, working, or just hanging out are much more fun with a pal. Your cat will be one of the best friends you could ever hope to have. It will share your quiet times and your busy ones. It will make you laugh, and make you feel loved and needed. Remember, a happy, healthy pet is a great pal. Take good care of your cat and it will take the best care of you.

Index

animal shelters 12

bedding 14, 18
bell 15
body harness 29
body language 44–47
bowls 15, 23, 35, 36
breeders 13

cat flap 17
cat grass 33
cat kennel 37
catnip 16, 33
cat-proofing home 17
cat run 17
check-ups 13, 38, 40
collars 15

dangerous foods 23
dangerous plants 33
drowning 17

ears 12, 27, 39, 40
eyes 12, 25, 27, 39, 40

feeding 22
fleas 38
food 22
   dispenser 36

grooming 24–27
grooming tools 24

hairball 27, 41
health checks 13, 38, 40
hissing 44

illness, signs of 41
introductions to
   another cat 19
   your dog 19
   your family 18–19

litter box 7, 14, 15, 17, 20, 21, 35

microchips 7, 13, 15
mixed breeds 11

neutering 7, 12, 42
nose 12

pedigree papers 12, 13
picking up kitten and cat 28
playing 30, 31, 32
purebreds 8–10

queen 42

records 13, 37
rules 20

safety 17, 29
scratching post 15, 16, 45

sense of smell 21, 45
settling in 18

tabby 8–11
tags 15
tail 27, 29
ticks 38
toilet training 21
tom 42
toys 30, 31, 32
training on a leash 29
travel 34
travel kit 35
travel stress 35
traveling box 18, 34, 35, 41
treats 20, 22

vaccinations 12, 13, 37, 39, 43

water, drinking 14, 15, 22, 23, 34, 36
   dispenser 36
worming 13, 39